Dora Sneaks Another Squeak

by Olivia Tartan

Thanks

Thank you to my support team who have helped me through this journey of writing my first children's book series. Tasmyn, for believing in me and connecting me to Matt and the PublishU team. Kirsty, Chantelle and Fiona for your proof reading, feedback and love and support. Nick for all your amazing illustration work, bringing Dora's stories alive. Matt for all your encouragement and showing me that I do have the ability to write a book.
A special thanks to my parents for being so supportive and amazing throughout this journey and to bounce ideas off.
And lastly, thank you for everyone who has bought my book and share the love of animals everywhere.

Dora is back for another adventure and her Master has surrendered to all of Dora's cuddles which are so soft and tender.

Now, let's get to Dora's comeback before she unpacks those NOISES from where her tail sits back.

Dora's last adventure had her sneaking and squeaking which got us all reading everything that she was revealing. Dora can eat her treat but first she must sit tall and neat and it's not long until she starts to speak with that sound of a SQUEAK!

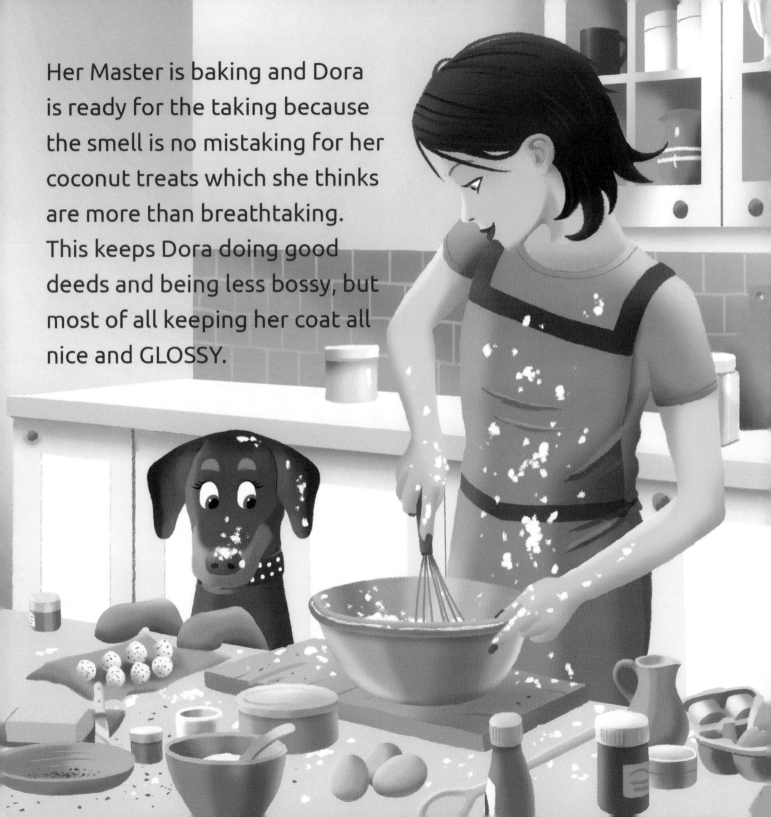

Her Master is baking and Dora is ready for the taking because the smell is no mistaking for her coconut treats which she thinks are more than breathtaking. This keeps Dora doing good deeds and being less bossy, but most of all keeping her coat all nice and GLOSSY.

The clock strikes on that hour and we now must power to that place with all the flowers because nothing makes her prouder than seeing her friends around her.

As Dora arrives at the park, she is so excited she tries not to bark, but all of a sudden, she lets out a FART.

Dora embraces all those familiar faces she plays with and knows what their game is.

Dora is up to her tricks and is ready to pinch their tennis ball before they can flinch. Dora has a bit of a reputation that gets her into all sorts of situations. Dora gathers the balls in front of her and has everyone's attention now that their ball game is in suspension.

There is more to unpack within this tailback pack. There is Rusty, Java, Harry, Archie, Georgia and don't forget Hazel who have all come out to be PLAYFUL.

Dora is up to her tricks and this time she flicks the water bowl over with so much control and makes her Master angry, like that was her main goal. Her Master refills the water bowl and Dora strolls back to flick it again, showing us she's out of CONTROL!

Dora is now off her game because she has spotted someone to tame, eating a banana which she is ready to claim. No-one can dispute that this is definitely her favourite FRUIT!

Dora takes time to check up on her Master who is picking up Dora's poo after going to the loo. "EWWW" but no one would approve if your shoes got glued to the poo. So it's the right thing to do, to pick up the poo.

Back at home, Dora thinks of the extreme and it's off to the next mischievous scheme. Dora is out in garden, dragging the flowers and herbs across the yard, left then right, deciding her work here is final.

Dora is a dog that needs a lot of attention because her next invention is to pull your clothes from where the clothes line is stationed. She gives them a toss out on the lawn like this is her latest inspiration.

Dora is finding more of your things to hide on the side and if you're missing a sock don't forget to check the flock that she has stocked.

The best thing about Dora, is not just her sweet look but she eats anything even if you're a bad cook. She studies you in the kitchen and is ready in position looking at you for permission if you could make something in addition.

If Dora had a diary, it would say that she can eat a variety of fruits, vegetables and fish. A healthy diet for your dog will give them vitamins by the dozen but definitely NO ONIONS.

Dora lets out a loud SQUEAK and looks back at her Master as if "it wasn't me"! But in reality, she's saying she's ready to EAT!

Dora is a messy eater and gets her dinner on the wall, floor and even on her jaw. She moves her bowl as if it was going on a stroll.

This canine even MUNCHES and CRUNCHES on a carrot a day so her teeth stay more than okay and never decay.

After dinner this girl is no beginner, Dora always aims to play these games and has no shame when she sneaks a PEEK even when she is the one to seek. Dora finds you and comes at you with so much bounce that suddenly she lets out something sounding more PRONOUNCED.

Our love is unconditional even if we have been apart,
reuniting with a waggling tail warms the heart.
Because Dora missed you at every moment and celebrates
your arrival with a little DANCE COMPONENT.

About the Author

Olivia Tartan is a newly published author of children's books based in Brisbane, Australia.
Passionate about animals and her adoring dog Dora,
Olivia is always learning healthy recipes to cook for her dog and enjoys getting outdoors socialising Dora.

Other Books

Printed in Great Britain
by Amazon